It is playtime.
Ravi has lost his bal

Everyone looks for Ravi's ball.

"Is it here?"
asks Sam.

contents.

No!

"Is it under here?" asks Ben.

THIS WAY UP!

No!
THIS WAY UP!

"Is it behind
here?"
asks Jojo.

No!
LUNCH BOX

"Where is it?" asks Miss Cherry.

"I can see it" says Billy.

"Over there!"